GW00361187

1 Outside the Duck in the Pond, Kenton Lane, Harrow Weald, about 1910

2 *Next page* Outside the Grand Theatre in Islington about 1900

Victorian and Edwardian

MIDDLESEX

from old photographs

Introduction and commentaries by

IAN MURRAY

B.T. BATSFORD LTD
LONDON

ACKNOWLEDGEMENTS

The author and publishers wish to thank the following for their kindness in allowing the photographs in this book to be reproduced, and in particular wish to thank the various Local History and Reference Librarians involved for their willing co-operation and assistance in the selection of the photographs and for much helpful information: London Borough of Enfield Libraries Service for figs 27, 28, 40, 41, 68, 108 and 140; London Borough of Hounslow Library Service for figs 9–15, 24, 25, 42, 69, 89, 92, 102, 106, 107, 109, 111, 122, 132–134 and 136; Hillingdon Borough Libraries for figs 5, 8, 17, 54, 64, 70, 72, 83, 90, 96, 99, 101, 123, 124 and 135; London Borough of Harrow Libraries for figs 1, 3, 16, 67, 71, 75, 85, 87, 88, 104, 119, 125 and 129–131; London Borough of Barnet Libraries Department for figs 18–21, 26, 43, 55–58, 84, 91 and 110; London Borough of Brent Library Service for figs 7, 22, 23, 45, 59, and 60; London Borough of Richmond upon Thames Libraries for figs 29, 30, 44, 76, 115, 116, 126 and 127; London Borough of Haringey Libraries, Museum and Arts Service for figs 4, 6, 31–36, 46–51, 62, 63, 65, 66, 73, 74, 77, 78, 80, 82, 86, 93–95, 100, 103, 105, 112, 114, 118, 120, 121, 128, 137–139, 141 and 140; London Borough of Camden Libraries and Arts Service for figs 37–39 and 79; London Borough of Islington Libraries Department for figs 2, 52, 81, 97 and 142; London Borough of Ealing Libraries for figs 53 and 61; Gunnersbury Park Museum for fig 117.

First published 1977
Copyright Ian Murray 1977

Set in Monophoto Apollo by
Servis Filmsetting Ltd, Manchester
Printed by
The Anchor Press Ltd, Tiptree, Essex
for the Publishers B.T. Batsford Ltd
4 Fitzhardinge Street, London W1H 0AH

ISBN 0 7134 0181 8

CONTENTS

Acknowledgements

Introduction

3   F. Stiles' travelling stores in Harrow in about 1900

4 Children with servants at the rear of a house in Tottenham, photographed by the Hunnings about 1870

INTRODUCTION

The photographs in this book have been selected from public library collections within the old County of Middlesex and include a number from that part of it which became the County of London in 1888. Librarians in Middlesex as elsewhere showed an early interest in local photographs and those published here out of the many thousands examined give some indication of the extent and value of their collections. The photographs illustrate the changes which have taken place in the county within the last hundred years and at the same time reflect its social and economic character, though inevitably coverage of the area is by no means uniform or complete. Places and subjects which would have been of interest today were only patchily recorded, or photographs of them have not survived, while certain parts of the county were completely ignored. Willesden, for example, received much attention but neighbouring Wembley, probably because of its insignificance until recent years, was neglected.

Middlesex, despite its favourable position in relation to the capital, does not seem to have produced or attracted any of the pioneers of photography and little survives prior to 1860 apart from some ambrotype portraits of an Uxbridge family held by Hillingdon Libraries. Photographs of the 1860s and early 70s are again uncommon in public collections with the exception of some from Hornsey, Tottenham and Willesden, and even when technical advances brought the camera within the reach of the general public it was usually the larger centres of population and wealth which were photographed rather than the remoter rural areas. In general, the photographers of the period were more interested in recording well-known local features and public events than the details of contemporary social life which often emerge incidentally. Local authority institutions such as the fire brigade were popular subjects and also social and public events of which the Diamond Jubilee celebrations and those for the coronation of Edward VII were perhaps the most common. The opening of public buildings and services, railway stations, public houses, churches, high streets and other local landmarks received attention and in particular the new tramways. There is, therefore, little to compare with the work of Paul Martin who in London in the 1890s consciously recorded the street life and ordinary people of his time, except for a few photographs by amateurs in the urban areas of the county who took up photography as a hobby with the arrival of cheaper and more efficient cameras. Most photographers at that time neglected the humbler scenes and it was

5   An outing from St Andrew's Church, Uxbridge, before 1914

usually local authority photographers who recorded the living conditions of the poor and other important aspects of the age in the course of their official duties.

These, however, are the complaints of the modern historian and it is unrewarding to blame contemporary photographers for not having achieved exactly what posterity would have wished.

During the years which these photographs illustrate the county changed radically. At the beginning of Victoria's reign Middlesex was still mostly rural and had its own character, dependent economically upon London as it was. Outside the metropolitan area there were few large towns, and small villages and hamlets predominated, their buildings usually of weatherboard or brick. Its farms specialised in the production of dairy produce and hay for the London market; market gardening and brickmaking were also important. Numerous local crafts connected with a rural economy thrived, as did boat building along the Thames, but industry was uncommon except in certain places such as Brentford and in the valleys of the Lea and Colne where water power and transport were available. In these areas, flour, oilseed and gunpowder mills had been founded, the mills of Uxbridge being particularly famous, while rubber was processed in Tottenham and the manufacture of crape, which prospered with the fashion for full mourning, was carried on at Ponders End and Tottenham.

Middlesex was therefore eminent neither as a manufacturing nor as an agricultural county. Its importance lay in its close proximity to London and from an early date parts of it were favoured by members of the court and the merchant classes who wished to live conveniently near the centre of government and commerce. Highgate attracted many such residents, and what in the sixteenth century had been a wayside hamlet on the Great North Road soon became because of its healthy elevation a popular suburb of London. The same is true of Chiswick and Twickenham along the Thames, which had easy access to the City by water. In the nineteenth century, with a general increase in trade and prosperity, the process accelerated. City merchants moved into the rural county in large numbers where they could set up as squires and lead the life of country gentlemen. There was scarcely a village in Middlesex without its complement of big houses which offered employment to the local people and prestige to their inhabitants. The small hamlet of Crouch End, for example, with a population of only a few hundred in mid century, possessed at least three. Topsfield Hall and Crouch Hall were occupied by a bristle merchant and iron founder respectively and both were pulled down at the end of the century when the value of their grounds as building land persuaded the owners to sell up. The Priory at the foot of the Alexandra Park had been built for only 60 years.

Towards the end of the century however the county was beginning to lose its rural character as well as its individuality, a development that did not escape the notice of contemporaries. As early as 1862 it was noted (of Edgware) in Kelly's *Post Office Directory for Middlesex*: 'Like the generality of ancient towns near London all its importance as a market town has long since vanished and it may now be ranked among the suburban districts of the metropolis'. Most of Middlesex was then still rural, but London was beginning to expand physically into the countryside and by the 1870s the northern suburbs extended as far as Hackney, Upper Holloway, Hampstead, Paddington and Hammersmith. In 1888 the creation of the County of London had robbed Middlesex of much of its ancient territory and the suburbs continued to expand into what remained. By 1914, Tottenham, Edmonton and Enfield in the Lea valley had been absorbed as well as Hornsey to the east while at the same time some of the outlying towns such as Harrow and Uxbridge had greatly increased in population as the result of suburban railway building. The final blow came after the First World War with the extension of the London tubes, and in 1964 with the creation of Greater London and the extinction of Middlesex as an administrative county the spread of the London suburbs into the old county was complete.

The mass growth of the Middlesex suburbs took place after about 1880, but earlier in the century the beginnings of the process can be discerned as middle class Londoners, following the example of the rich, moved into the outlying villages and built villas in rural surroundings, usually on the main roads out of London. Hounslow, for example, which suffered a decline with the disappearance of the coaching traffic is described in 1862 thus: 'A new class of inhabitants and improved society are producing wonders in the way of general improvements . . . its gravelly soil and proverbial salubrity, combined with excellent and cheap railway accommodation, render Hounslow a favourable residence for gentlemen connected with the metropolis.' The movement was prompted by a desire to live in a respectable rural neighbourhood where a certain social standing could be enjoyed and also to escape from the unhealthiness of London and proximity to the poor in the slums. When suburban development gathered momentum, areas in the county already popular and served by good railway communications expanded and in the process certain districts became more exclusive than others. The original northern suburbs of Stoke Newington, Upper Holloway and Paddington were to some extent abandoned by the well-to-do in favour of remoter parts of the county, though some suburbs such as Tottenham and Edmonton had always been working and lower-middle class. Neighbouring Hornsey and Wood Green, because they stood on higher and less easily developed ground were considered to be higher up the social scale. The final stage was the disappearance of the remaining rural areas, such as Ruislip, Finchley, Hendon and Edgware, so that today in most parts of the county farms and country houses have given way to brick terraces and housing estates.

The factors which caused the expansion were numerous and interacting, the most obvious being a simple increase in the population of London which forced people to seek homes further afield, but the growth could not have occurred without the building of suburban railways which made the development of outlying villages into commuter suburbs possible in the first place. Here, cheapness of travel played an important part. High fares meant exclusive suburbs, but on the other hand the return fare from Enfield to Liverpool Street on a line opened in 1872 was as low as a shilling a week on workmen's trains. The result was a great increase in population and house building along the line, much to the regret of those already living in the area, who complained in the local papers of the likely increase in poverty and disease and a consequent rise in the rates. The destruction of housing in inner London as a result of railway building and a displacement of population also contributed to the movement outwards as did a general desire to escape from high rents and overcrowding in the metropolis.

The photographs which survive of Middlesex and its people during this period are a source of much local information as well as pleasure in its own right, and their value is therefore twofold. On one level the local historian can use certain topographical photographs together with other sources such as Ordnance Survey maps and official records in order to trace the development of the area he is concerned with, for general views and street scenes are helpful in establishing the dates of vanished buildings and those of new streets, houses and shops. In addition they sometimes provide otherwise unrecorded information on alterations to buildings, but apart from such instances historic photographs rarely contain information which does not already exist elsewhere in the form of rate books, maps and directories.

The second level of interest, though not of course separate, is social and accounts for the current popularity of historic photographs. Following the invention of photo-

6 The Three Jolly Butchers in Wood Green High Road after 1904 when the electric trams arrived. It has since been rebuilt

graphy, it has become possible for the first time to examine people, places and events over the past 130 years and to know exactly what they looked like. The ability to do so closes the gap between past and present and means that aspects of recent history can be grasped more easily. Photographs illuminate facts which are known from other sources but cannot be fully realized without the aid of a neutral witness. They show clearly, for example, the real difference in dress and in living standards between rich and poor, and the importance attached, in certain social classes, to dressing correctly for the occasion.

The fascination of looking at the past is common to scholar and layman alike, but it would be misleading to suggest that all photographs give an unbiased account of it or are complete in themselves. They leave much unsaid and the significance of what is depicted has often to be explained by reference to other historical sources. A photograph of a train or tram may be of interest in itself as an early means of transport but requires further information to put it in historical context. The camera can also lie in the sense that the reality behind the photograph may differ from what it seems to represent. The subject chosen by the photographer will reflect his predilections and more generally the taste and manners of the period and may not portray with absolute truth and accuracy the reality of life at the time. The rural charms of Middlesex shown in some of these photographs appeal to an urban generation who may regret the changes that have taken place, but it would be a mistake to believe that we have somehow left behind a golden age when for many people the reverse may be true. The variable quality of early photographs contributes to this attitude. A faint or blurred image gives an impression of unreality and of past history, though a good clear print conveys with absolute clarity the modernity of streets and buildings at the time.

A common reaction to some of the earlier photographs is one of surprise at the stiffness and formality of the poses which may reinforce notions about the nature of Victorian and Edwardian society, although in many cases the unkempt appearance of the men may be an antidote to an unduly romantic view of the era. It is possible also to become sentimental and to enthuse over the charms of many of them and the tranquillity and order of a vanished age which the photographs seem to reflect. This is a case of being deceived by the image for the reality was no doubt different. The reason for this reaction probably lies in the primitive techniques at first employed. A wet plate exposure took at least eight seconds and earlier processes much longer, so it is hardly surprising that most subjects seem very serious and hardly ever smile. The necessity to remain quite still during the lengthy exposure discouraged spontaneity, and besides, photography was at first such a novel and unfamiliar experience that many people would become inhibited in front of the camera. It accounts also for the self-conscious poses and the curiosity which brought people to the front door if a photographer was in the street.

Photography was well established artistically and commercially by the 1850s, but there were as late as 1862 only 11 photographic artists, as they were significantly called, in the county outside the metropolis, three in Hammersmith, two in Hackney and Stoke Newington, and one each in Harrow, Staines, Brentford and Twickenham. A large proportion of this number had set up in the new London suburbs where clearly a market for their services existed among the middle class families settled there. These photographers engaged mainly in commercial studio portraiture, for the new medium was at first regarded as a cheap alternative to portrait painting, particularly in miniature. Little of their work seems to have survived, although one photograph by Edmund Goshawk of Harrow is of great interest. Goshawk is listed in the 1862 Directory as a hairdresser and photographer, an unlikely combination at first sight, though doubtless his hairdressing business brought him into contact with prospective clients for the camera. On 1 June 1866 he was commissioned to photograph part of the ancient wall surrounding the Manor of Flambards which was shortly to be demolished. According to the *Harrow Gazette and General Advertiser*, 'This interesting feature . . . is very shortly to be pulled down. . . . At the request of the purchaser, Mr Goshawk has taken two excellent photographs of it, so that when it shall become a thing of the past . . . those who come after us shall know what that part of Harrow was in our time'. This early example of the photographic recording of architectural monuments predates by many years the North Middlesex Photographic Society's survey of North Middlesex which aimed at the recording of the most important buildings of the area. A photographic survey of Ealing was also sponsored by the Public Library in the early years of this century.

With two important exceptions, however, the quality of surviving early photographs does not seem to be high. The first exception is George Shadbolt who photographed the countryside of Hornsey and the surrounding districts in the 1860s, although nothing of his life is known. In Tottenham, the firm of Hunnings who are listed as stationers in 1862 and later turned to printing, took up commercial photography after that date though examples of their work survive from the 1850s. The firm is still in existence though the printing works were moved some years ago from Tottenham High Road to Finsbury Park. As well as engaging in studio portraiture, the Hunnings also photographed local scenes and views and the result was a detailed record of the district just prior to its transformation into a commuter suburb in the late 1870s. Many hundreds of their glass plate negatives and original prints are now held by Haringey Libraries and include an unusual one of the photographers posing with their equipment. A member of the Winter family, possibly J. S. Winter, Senior Curate of Tottenham, was also active in the mid 1850s throughout the south-east of England generally, experimenting in calotype and wet collodion.

The scarcity of surviving local photographs up to the 1870s has already been noted and can be explained by the difficulties of early photography. Techniques were at first so complicated and equipment so bulky and expensive that all but the most ardent and wealthy amateurs were deterred and the field was left largely to professionals of whom there were very few in Middlesex. All developing had to be done by the photographer, a drawback common to daguerrotype, calotype and wet collodion alike, although the latter was somewhat less complicated and attracted amateurs in large numbers. It was not until 1871, when the dry plate process was introduced and with it the hand-held camera, that photography came within reach of the general public. Dry plate negatives could be sent away to commercial firms for developing and printing and the cost of photography thus decreased. A further development was the Kodak roll film camera of 1888 with a much reduced exposure time so that the snapshot which recorded the social scene unobtrusively was possible.

The introduction of the half-tone screen process two years later enabled photographs to be printed in newspapers and picture postcards to be produced. Large numbers of these showing local scenes survive from all parts of Middlesex, a reminder of the days when communication by postcard was cheap and common, forming a valuable record of the growing suburbs. Local lantern slides are another important source.

From the 1890s, therefore, thousands of photographs were taken which, added to the earlier ones, provide a permanent record of Middlesex and its people. Some of the most interesting examples are presented here and it is hoped that they convey something of the character of the county in the recent past.

TOWNS AND VILLAGES

7 The premises of James Crook, the undertakers, between Messina Avenue and Palmerston Road in Kilburn High Road about 1880. The cycle is a Coventry tricycle introduced in 1876

8 Ickenham about 1900, then an agricultural village whose population of 364 in 1851 had risen to only 433 in 1921 despite its having been served by the Harrow and Uxbridge line since 1904

9 Market morning at Kew Bridge in 1893. The horse trough has recently been dismantled and re-assembled at Brentford in the cause of road improvements. Behind stands the Grand Junction Waterworks Company's Chiswick Pumping Station with an elegant standpipe tower, by Alexander Fraser (1867), now a museum of pumping machinery

10 Chiswick Mall, on the eastern side of Chiswick in the 1890s, with Thames spritsail barges moored on the banks of the river and Thorneycroft's Chiswick works in the background. Beyond is open country, mostly orchards and market gardens for which the area was famed. The Mall is late seventeenth and early eighteenth century in origin

11 Strand on the Green, Chiswick, in the 1860s with Kew Bridge in the background. The Strand consisted of a row of fishermen's cottages until the late eighteenth century, after which it became fashionable

12   The toll house and gate on Kew
Bridge, removed in 1873

13   *Below* Brentford High Street in 1892
looking towards Brentford Church,
rebuilt in 1764 with the fifteenth-
century tower retained. Brentford
was one of the few industrial centres
in Middlesex and claimed to be the
county's first town. The county
elections were traditionally held there

14 Church Walk, off Somerset Walk, Brentford in 1893, an unposed snapshot rare at so early a date

15 The Standard Inn, Half Acre, Brentford, demolished in 1897 and an example of the small beerhouse common in Middlesex towns before their development as London suburbs. The poster which advertises a Grenadier Guards' football match dates the photograph at 1896

16 The wall enclosing part of the
ancient manor of Flambards on the
east side of the London Road, Harrow,
and opposite the King's Head,
photographed on 1 June 1866 by
Edmund Goshawk, hairdresser and
photographer

17 *Right, above* Looking up Uxbridge
High Street towards St Margaret's
Church during the Diamond Jubilee
celebrations of 1897

18 *Right* The Green Man at
Whetstone on the Great North Road
in the 1870s. Whetstone was one of
the three main settlements of Finchley
and remained rural until after the
First World War. The name is found
in the fifteenth century, but its
derivation is uncertain

19 The Greyhound Inn next to St Mary's Church, Hendon, in the 1870s, since rebuilt. The occasion the photograph records is unknown

20 *Below* The Old King of Prussia at Church End, Finchley, about 1890; now, like so many of the weather-boarded inns of Middlesex, pulled down and rebuilt

21 Child's Hill, Cricklewood Lane, near the junction with Finchley Road about 1900. A contingent of the Boys' Brigade attracts attention

22 The Crown at Harlesden in 1877, showing from left to right, Mr Willis the local butcher armed with the tools of his trade, Mr Naylor the Assistant Overseer, Mr Price the grocer and other unidentified characters.

23 *Right, above* The Spotted Dog, Willesden Green, since rebuilt and now in the middle of an urban shopping parade. The poster advertising the extension of the Metropolitan railway to Harrow dates the photograph at 1880

24 *Right* Hounslow turnpike and tollgate in the 1860s. The Staines Road was freed from toll in 1872

25 *Next page* The parish cage or lock-up at Cranford in the 1880s

NOTICES

26 The Chandos Arms, Edgware High Street, in the 1870s

27 Church Road, Edmonton, showing the site of the Charles Lamb Institute in 1903. William Shearer, headmaster of The Latymer School is shown. Albert Monk was an ex-Hackney parochial schoolboy who made good

28 The Waggon and Horses, Chase Side, Southgate, about 1885

29 *Right, above* Teddington Lock and Weir under flood about 1890

30 *Right* Laurel Lodge in Heath Road, Twickenham in 1875, showing Lilian Ashton and Isobel Martin in the garden

31 Tottenham High Road about 1890, near the entrance to Bruce Grove and showing the George and Vulture Inn, a popular resort in the eighteenth and nineteenth centuries, now demolished. The site is occupied by a supermarket

32 *Below* The premises of Stocks and Peasgood, plumbers, of Tottenham High Road with some of their workmen. The photograph was taken by the Hunnings in the 1860s

33 Shops at 41 and 43 Hornsey High Street in about 1890. These typical weatherboarded buildings were later pulled down to make way for a suburban shopping parade

34 The old Hope and Anchor in Tottenham Lane, Hornsey, in the 1880s. It was later rebuilt on a grander scale when the district was developed as a commuter suburb

35 Edgware High Street about 1900

36 The Bull Inn at the south end of Tottenham Green, taken after the rebuilding of 1865. During demolition in 1939 the timber frames of the original Tudor building were discovered. This print was taken from an original glass negative and shows the lines caused by cracks in the emulsion

37 *Left* The top of Hampstead High Street before 1886, when many of these buildings were demolished in the course of town improvements

38 *Left, below* Hampstead Heath near the Spaniards Road in the 1870s showing the excavations for sand and gravel which account for the level of the road today above the surrounding Heath. The preservation of Hampstead Heath as an open space was the result of a lengthy struggle between local residents and the Lord of the Manor, Sir Thomas Wilson, who wished to enclose it for building purposes

39 Whitestone Pond on Hampstead Heath in the 1890s. The Pond, at about 440 feet above sea level Hampstead's highest point, is entirely artificial, and is so called from a nearby milestone

THE GROWING SUBURBS

Baker Street, Enfield.

40 Preparing the track for the trams through Enfield Town opposite the George Inn in 1909

41 The corner of Churchbury Road and Baker Street, Enfield, about 1907. The shop on the right is that of H. Purchase, plumber and decorator, while on the far corner is Garner's the clothiers

HIGH ROAD, CHISWICK. 210

42 Chiswick High Road before 1901, with work progressing on the erection of overhead cables for the electric trams which arrived in that year

43 The start of an outing from the George at Finchley about 1900

44 Station Road, Twickenham in 1905

45 The Queen's Arms, Kilburn High Road in 1886. Kilburn was on the fringe of the built-up area of London in about 1860 and was engulfed soon after

46 A horse bus passing Crouch End Clock Tower, completed in 1895 to commemorate H. R. Williams, the preserver of Highgate Woods and an important personality in the development of modern Crouch End

47 *Below* Looking down Crouch End
Hill towards the Broadway and
Dunn's the bakers. The houses on the
left have been replaced by the
telephone exchange, and the building
on the right-hand corner, then the
village smithy, by the National
Westminster Bank

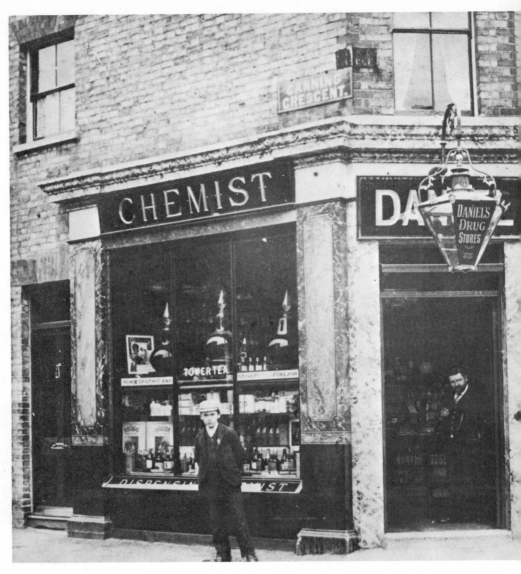

48 The corner of Canning Crescent and Wood Green High Road about 1900

49 Crouch End Broadway about 1890 looking towards Topsfield Hall, which was demolished in 1896 to make way for Topsfield Parade

50 Palmerston Crescent, Wood Green, in 1903. A part of Tottenham until 1888, Wood Green was thought to be socially superior and is described in 1894 thus: 'This pleasant suburb boasts many handsome villa residences occupied by a better class than those who live in Tottenham proper'

51 An unposed snapshot in Green
Lanes, Harringay, about 1890.
Williamson's potteries are on the
right

52 Advertising at Paskell's cycle
shop at 146 Seven Sisters Road about
1904

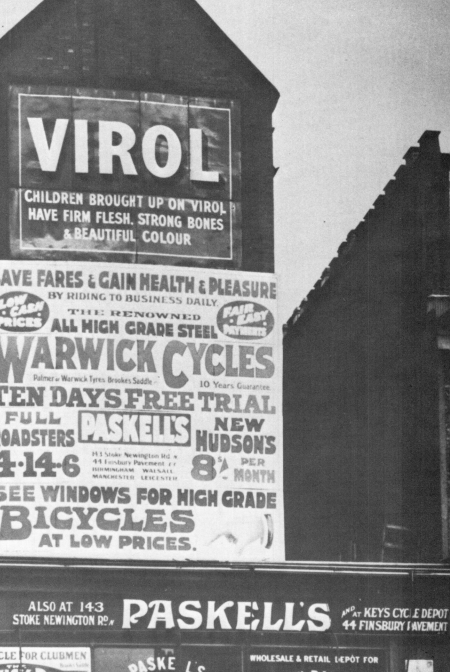

VIROL

CHILDREN BROUGHT UP ON VIROL HAVE FIRM FLESH. STRONG BONES & BEAUTIFUL COLOUR

SAVE FARES & GAIN HEALTH & PLEASURE
BY RIDING TO BUSINESS DAILY.

LOW CASH PRICES

THE RENOWNED
ALL HIGH GRADE STEEL

EASY TERMS PAYMENTS

WARWICK CYCLES

Palmer or Warwick Tyres Brookes Saddle

10 Years Guarantee

TEN DAYS FREE TRIAL

FULL
ROADSTERS
4·14·6

PASKELL'S

143 Stoke Newington Rd N
44 Finsbury Pavement EC
BIRMINGHAM WALSALL
MANCHESTER LEICESTER

NEW
HUDSON'S
8/- PER
MONTH

SEE WINDOWS FOR HIGH GRADE
BICYCLES
AT LOW PRICES.

GET OFF THAT TRAM!
IT WILL NEVER BE YOURS
The same money brought to Paskell's
FOUR PENCE A DAY.
WILL BUY you a BICYCLE

146A ALSO AT 143
STOKE NEWINGTON RD. N
PASKELL'S
AND AT KEYS CYCLE DEPOT
44 FINSBURY PAVEMENT

THE BICYCLE FOR CLUBMEN
WARWICK ROYAL
THE MACHINE FOR PLEASURE
GET CATALOGUES NOW.

PASKELL'S
CYCLE DEPOT
ALSO
COVENTRY, BIRMINGHAM
AND BRANCHES.
HEAD OFFICE
BIRMINGHAM

WHOLESALE & RETAIL DEPOT FOR
NEW RAPID
.8.0 1 5.0
CYCLES
25 YEARS REPUTATION

ALL THE WORLD + HIS WIFE
NEW HUDSON
CYCLES
ALL THE WORLD + HIS WIFE
NEW HUDSON
CYCLES

THE COUNTRYSIDE

53 Rural Acton; the Cock and Crown yard, demolished in 1909 to make way for Crown Street

54 Setting off on the milk round from Oak Farm, Uxbridge, in about 1900

55 *Above* Edgewarebury Lane,
Edgware, in about 1904. A rural scene
since transformed

56 The Plough Inn at Highwood
Hill, Mill Hill, one of the district's
original hamlets, about 1900. Mill Hill
was not built up until after 1920

57 Goldbeater's Farm, Burnt Oak,
n 1877. The farm stood south-west of
Mill Hill station and was demolished
n 1928

58 The Manor House, Finchley, on East End Road in about 1900. The building still survives as a convent school

59 Bramley's Farm, Willesden, in the 1860s. Although near to London, Willesden remained rural until the end of the nineteenth century

60 Rural Cricklewood, looking towards Shoot Up Hill. The carriage belongs to Miss Metcalfe, a resident of Richmond Villa, Cricklewood in the 1870s. She is seen taking a constitutional beside it

61 Hunt's Farm, Yeading Lane,
Northolt, in about 1903

62 *Top* View from the top of Muswell Hill in the 1870s before the development of the district, showing the Green Man and the entrance to the railway station, opened in 1873

63 *Above* Haymaking at Highgate about 1890

TIME OFF

64 An Uxbridge girl practising golf about 1910

65 The River Lea frozen over with the Ferryboat Inn in the background, 1893. The inn was a popular holiday resort until the late nineteenth century, a nearby attraction being Day's Dancing Grounds

66 The Sluice House on the New
River in 1869, near the present
Finsbury Park. The site is now
Wilberforce Road, the course of the
river having since been diverted. It
was then a popular angling centre

67 Stanmore cricket team about 1890

68 At the foot of Lavender Hill, Enfield, about 1900. E. Brown was a supplier of sideshows at fêtes in the Enfield district

69 The steam launch *Cardinal Wolsey* passing under Kew Bridge in August 1913

RuislIP SPORTS
1908   WinnerS of
Ladies EGG + Spoon RACe

70   The winner of the egg and spoon race at Ruislip Sports in 1908

71   Dancing bear performing in the Harrow Road, Wealdstone, in 1896. The site is near the modern Civic Centre

72 A carefully posed group at The Poplars, a fashionable Ruislip tea house, in about 1890

73 Racing at the Alexandra Palace in 1896. The course, known locally as the frying pan, was opened in 1868. It was closed and the grandstand demolished some years ago

74 Taking a corner at Tottenham Hotspurs ground in Northumberland Park in 1895. This was the original ground opened in 1888 and takings at the first match were only 17 shillings. The second drew a crowd of 350, but by the time of the move to the present ground in 1899, gates were around the 6,000 mark

75 Harrow Rovers Football Club in about 1890, photographed outside the pavilion in Roxborough Road Recreation Ground

76 *Right* Boating at Teddington Lock about 1890

77 *Right, below* A croquet match in Tottenham in the 1860s

78 *Next page* The start of a race at the cycling track in the grounds of Nightingale Hall, Wood Green, in 1896. The track existed from 1896 to 1900, when the estate was built over

79 *Left* Behind Jack Straw's Castle on Hampstead Heath about 1870. The area had been a popular holiday resort for many years, but a connection with Jack Straw and the Peasants' Revolt has never been authenticated

80 *Left, below* A mis-spent youth: billiards in The Greyhound, Phillip Lane, Tottenham, in 1901. The faint lettering on the board reads 'Success to the Spurs' which would date the photograph at this year when Spurs beat Sheffield United in the FA Cup Final

81 An entry in the 1904 Hornsey Carnival outside The Shaftesbury in Hornsey Rise

GREAT EVENTS

82 Inside Blandford Hall in
Alexandra Park, Wood Green. The
occasion was a gathering of colonial
troops to mark the coronation of
Edward VII

83 A dinner for old people in
Uxbridge Market House to celebrate
the Diamond Jubilee of 1897

4 Coach and horses on the frozen Welsh Harp in 1895. The reservoir was formed in 1838 by damming the Brent to supply water for the Grand Junction Canal

86 *Next page* A double wedding in Tottenham in the 1860s, photographed by the Hunnings

85 Edward VII visits Harrow in 1905

87 Pinner Fair in 1908, a nineteenth-century revival of a medieval tradition

88 Coronation celebrations in Pinner in 1911 – the horse and cart parade with the fifteenth-century tower of the church of St John the Baptist in the background. The back belongs to Farmer Gregory

89 One of the two Volunteer Service Companies of the Middlesex Regiment leaving Brentford Station for the Boer War either in March 1900 or May 1901. These were territorials who volunteered for active service. Although armed with the modern Lee Metford rifles, they still went to war in scarlet tunics

90 Empire Day celebrations at West
Drayton, 1913

91 Diamond Jubilee celebrations in
Sunny Hill Fields, looking towards
Hendon Church, 1897

92 The Thames frozen over at
Brentford, 4 January 1891

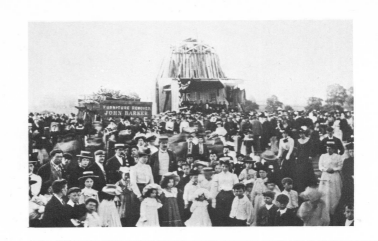

93   A bonfire in Downhills Fields,
Tottenham, to celebrate the coronation
of Edward VII

94   Beating the bounds of Tottenham
in 1886 along the River Lea, which
forms the eastern boundary of the
parish

95 Preparing for an ascent of the balloon *Eclipse* from Bruce Castle Park, Tottenham, on the occasion of the Tottenham and Edmonton Industrial Exhibition of 1891

96 *Below* Browne's premises in Uxbridge High Street decorated for the coronation of Edward VII. The business was listed as early as 1862

97 *Right* A float illustrating 'Justice' in an Islington pageant of 1902

98 *Right, below* Lord's: the luncheon interval during the Eton v. Harrow match of 1902

GETTING ABOUT

99   A London United Tramways 'W'
type tram outside the Adam and Eve
at Hayes in 1904. The band on the
top deck celebrates the extension of
the electric service from Southall to
Uxbridge through Hayes in that year

100   The tollgate on the Archway
Road near the present Archway
Tavern about 1870. The old Archway
visible in the distance was built by
Nash in 1813 and was replaced in 1900
by the modern bridge

101 The first train through Ruislip station on the Metropolitan Uxbridge branch in July 1904

102 One of the West London Omnibus Company's horse trams on the Shepherds Bush to Chiswick route, opened in 1883. The line passed into the hands of the London United Tramways Company in 1894 and was electrified in 1901

103 A steam tram passing along Tottenham High Road at some time between 1885 and 1891. The North London Omnibus Company operated a steam service during these years, but it was never successful and the company afterwards reverted to horse trams. It is not clear why the man is clinging to the front of the engine

104 Harrow and Wealdstone Station in about 1913 showing motor buses run by the London and Northwestern Railway Company to Watford Station. By 1912 the Company's suburban service had reached Harrow and was extended to Watford in the following year. The bus service was a temporary measure for the convenience of passengers

105 *Next page* Matthews Brothers cycle shop at 96, West Green Road, Tottenham, in 1896

AT WORK

106 A forge at Cranford about 1904

107 Unloading spritsail barges near Kew Bridge in 1893. Once common on the Thames, these craft had a shallow draught and were therefore extremely manoeuvrable. The leaboard, clearly visible, was lowered to form a moveable keel which prevented the barge from drifting

108 *Left, above* Hill's Nursery,
Crescent Road, Edmonton, about 1900.
The glass house industry in the Lea
valley became important towards the
end of the last century

109 *Left* The Royal Brewery Yard,
Brentford, in the 1870s

110 Laying tram tracks in Finchley
High Road opposite Ravensdale
Avenue, 1909

111   The launch of the torpedo gunboat *Speedy* from Thorneycroft's Chiswick Yard in 1893. The firm specialised in this type of vessel

12 Milk float in Truro Avenue, Wood Green, in 1908. David Sexton is listed in the directories as cowkeeper of Stuart Crescent

113   Female employees at Ponders
End crape works in the 1860s

114   J. A. Prestwich's works in Northumberland Park, Tottenham, before 1914. The firm's best
known product was the one-stroke JAP motorcycle engine

115   Making up Sherland Road,
Twickenham, about 1880. The man
with outstretched arms is George
Ramsay, Surveyor to the Twickenham
Local Board

116   Laying water mains in Heath Road, Twickenham, 1903

117 Bann's tannery, Brentford,
about 1880

118 A butcher's shop in Tottenham
High Road about 1870. The original
mount is labelled 'Christmas show of
meat', and is signed by W. J.
Hunnings

SCHOOLS

119   Outside the Headmaster's house,
Harrow School, in 1885

120   Infants' Class at White Hart
Lane School, Wood Green, in 1906.
The stepped class room was a feature
of early local authority schools and
enabled the teacher to keep an eye
on every pupil

121 Girls of Tottenham Blue School, so called from the colour of the pupils' dresses, photographed at the Tottenham and Edmonton Industrial Exhibition of 1865. The Blue School was a charity school which prepared girls for domestic service

122 Pupils at Isleworth Blue School in the 1860s. William S. Card was the Headmaster

123 Pupils at Mrs Cave's school in Uxbridge High Street celebrating Empire Day in 1904

124 Cricket team from the School of Industry for Girls, George Yard, Uxbridge, about 1892

THE PEOPLE

125 By a stile in Belmont, Harrow, in about 1905

126 A group outside the London City Mission in London Road, Twickenham, which was demolished in 1902 to make way for York Street

127 *Next page* Staff and customers at Heal's the farriers in Wharf Lane, Twickenham, about 1895

128 Two members of the Hunnings family of Tottenham in the 1860s, posing with their photographic equipment, which includes stereoscopic cameras and the chemicals necessary to produce a wet collodion photograph

129 William Warren Clowes, on the right, with the hose truck he invented in 1875. The photograph was taken in the late 1880s outside Harrow fire station

130 Mr Garner, a shepherd of Church
Farm, Pinner, in about 1900

131 A carter outside Winter's Supply
Stores in Wealdstone about 1900. The
shop adjoins the Duke of Edinburgh
public house

132 Jasper Price and Mrs Brent, country people from Cranford about 1880

133 *Left, below* Auntie Green outside her shop in Hounslow High Street in 1898

134 A group photographed at Chiswick Pumping Station about 1875

135   Pond's bakery van in Windsor Street, Uxbridge, about 1900

136   Staff at Isleworth station about 1880

137 The Morley children of 17, Hanover Road, Tottenham, about 1890

138 Spectators at the Ti-To-Tum Club, an athletics club in the grounds of Gothic House, St Ann's Road, Tottenham, about 1900

139 The Morley family about 1895

140 The Blue Lion Café in Fore
Street, Edmonton about 1910

141   A group at the rear of a house in Tottenham in the 1860s

142   The staff of Marriott's, the builders of Hornsey Rise, Islington, on their annual outing about 1904